W9-AZS-765

INVESTIGATE

Cocaine and Crack

LETHIAN

PUBLIC LIBRARY

INVESTIGATE

Marylou Ambrose
and
Veronica Deisler

E **Enslow Publishers, Inc.**
40 Industrial Road
Box 398
Berkeley Heights, NJ 07922
USA

http://www.enslow.com

Copyright © 2015 by Marylou Ambrose and Veronica Deisler

All rights reserved.

No part of this book may be reproduced by any means
without the written permission of the publisher.

Library of Congress Cataloging-in-Publication Data

Ambrose, Marylou.
   Investigate cocaine and crack / Marylou Ambrose and Veronica Deisler.
      pages cm.—(Investigate drugs)
   Summary: "Find out what cocaine and crack are, what happens when someone becomes addicted, and
     how the addiction is treated"—Provided by publisher.
   Includes bibliographical references and index.
   ISBN 978-0-7660-4255-1
   1. Cocaine—Juvenile literature. 2. Cocaine—Health aspects—Juvenile literature.
     3. Cocaine abuse—Juvenile literature. 4. Crack (Drug)—Health aspects—Juvenile literature. I.
   Deisler, Veronica. II. Title.
   RC568.C6A63 2015
   616.86'47—dc23

                2013018262

Future editions:
Paperback ISBN: 978-1-4644-0453-5   EPUB ISBN: 978-1-4645-1246-9
Single-User PDF ISBN: 978-1-4646-1246-6   Multi-User PDF ISBN: 978-0-7660-5878-1

Printed in the United States of America
052014 Lake Book Manufacturing, Inc., Melrose Park, IL
10 9 8 7 6 5 4 3 2 1

To Our Readers: We have done our best to make sure all Internet Addresses in this book were active and appropriate when we went to press. However, the author and the publisher have no control over and assume no liability for the material available on those Internet sites or on other Web sites they may link to. Any comments or suggestions can be sent by e-mail to comments@enslow.com or to the address on the back cover. Enslow Publishers, Inc., is committed to printing our books on recycled paper. The paper in every book contains 10% to 30% post-consumer waste (PCW).

♻ Enslow Publishers, Inc., is committed to printing our books on recycled paper. The paper in every book contains 10% to 30% post-consumer waste (PCW). The cover board on the outside of each book contains 100% PCW. Our goal is to do our part to help young people and the environment too!

Illustration Credits: AP Images/Bias Family, p. 37; AP Images/LM Otero, p. 8; AP Images/ Patrick McMullan Co., p. 58; Library of Congress, pp. 28 (left), 33; National Institutes of Health (NIH), p. 95; National Institute on Drug Abuse, p. 47; Shutterstock.com: Anton_Ivanov, pp. 26–27; antoshkaforever, p. 15; Joel Shawn, p. 24; ©Thinkstock: BananaStock, p. 71; Brookhaven National Laboratory, p. 51; Dieter Meyrl/iStock, p. 43; Dynamic Graphics/liquidlibrary, p. 17; Elliot Burlingham/iStock, p. 79; ivosar/iStock, p. 53; jtgray/iStock, p. 1; Lisa F. Young/iStock, p. 92; Micha Adamczyk/iStock, p. 61; moodboard, p. 49; Neil P. Mockford/Getty Images Entertainment, p. 74; roberthyrons/iStock, p. 86; RTimages/iStock, p. 30; Sohadiszno/iStock, p. 22; tolgakolcak/iStock, p. 63; Vladimir Melnik/iStock, p. 13; Wavebreak Media Ltd., pp. 54, 89; Wayne Abraham/iStock, pp. 3–5, 7, 21, 40, 56, 69, 83, 97–112; United States Drug Enforcement Agency, p. 10 (both); Wikipedia.com public domain image, pp. 28 (right), 34.

Cover Illustration: jtgray/iStock/©Thinkstock

YA
362.298

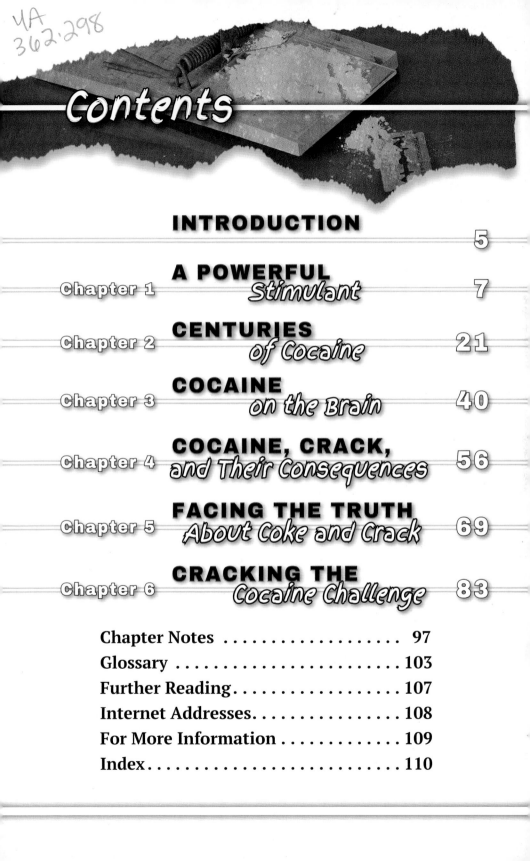

Contents

MIDLOTHIAN PUBLIC LIBRARY
14701 S. KENTON AVE.
MIDLOTHIAN, IL 60445

Introduction

The Incas believed that cocaine was a gift from the gods. Doctors in the nineteenth century thought it was a "miracle" drug. In the twentieth century, it became a popular "party" drug for the rich and famous. People thought cocaine was harmless. They were wrong.

Cocaine has caused two drug epidemics in the United States, one at the beginning and one at the end of the twentieth century. When crack, the crystal version of cocaine, came around in the 1980s, people who weren't rich could enjoy a cheaper form of the drug. But the reality was far from enjoyable. Crime became worse, families fell apart, careers were lost, and people died. Cocaine abuse still costs society billions of dollars every year.

This book gives you the truth about cocaine and crack cocaine. It shows where cocaine comes from and how it works in your body and your brain. It also explains what attracts people to cocaine and describes the latest methods for prevention and treatment. You'll learn that using cocaine really does have side effects. Plus, you'll find stories about actual people who've been affected by cocaine and crack addiction.

You or your friends may be faced with the decision to use cocaine someday. The information you find here will help you make an informed choice for yourself and the people you care about.

Chapter 1

A POWERFUL Stimulant

In December 2012, Josh Hamilton signed a five-year, $125-million deal with the Los Angeles Angels baseball team. At age thirty-one, the right fielder was on top of the world and at the top of his game. But seven years before, he'd been at rock bottom. Homeless, jobless, and suicidal, Josh had been addicted to cocaine.

Josh grew up in North Carolina, in a close-knit, athletic family. In high school, he focused on baseball, and never touched alcohol, tobacco, or other drugs. He signed with the Tampa Bay Devil Rays right out of high school, for a record $3.96 million bonus. He was voted Minor League Player of the Year in 2000.

Then in 2001, everything changed. Josh's parents had quit their jobs to travel with him and the team, and while

Los Angeles Angels' Josh Hamilton stands on the field during the ninth inning of a baseball game against the Texas Rangers on September 28, 2013, in Arlington, Texas.

in Florida, the three were in a car accident. Josh's mother was seriously injured and returned home with his father. Josh hurt his lower back and was put on the disabled list after only twenty-three games.

At age twenty, Josh was without his family for the first time in his life. He had lots of time to kill and plenty of money to spend. So he started hanging out with new friends who used drugs. Before long, Josh was experimenting with alcohol and cocaine.

Josh was hooked on cocaine immediately. He compared the rush he felt from his first line of coke to the thrill of hitting a baseball out of the park.

The managers of the Tampa Bay team knew something was wrong and ordered Josh to see a sports psychologist. Josh admitted he was using drugs and was sent to a drug rehab clinic. Unfortunately, he got angry and left before finishing the program.

Josh returned to the minor leagues, but then he hurt himself playing ball and needed surgery on his elbow and shoulder. He still hadn't given up alcohol and coke. In fact, he used to hide coke in his uniform during games. In 2003, he failed a drug test and was suspended. Finally, he failed so many tests he was barred from playing baseball for three years.

Shortly afterward, Josh reconnected with Katie Chadwick, a girl he'd known in high school. They got married in 2004. By this time, Josh had been in and out of rehab several times. He stayed sober for a while, but by the time his first daughter was born in 2005, Josh was using coke again. He pawned Katie's wedding ring and

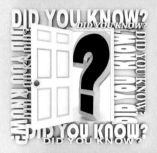
Cocaine is sold illegally in two chemical forms. One form is powder and the other is a solid chip, chunk, or rock, known as crack.

Freebase cocaine has been cooked in water with ammonia and ether.

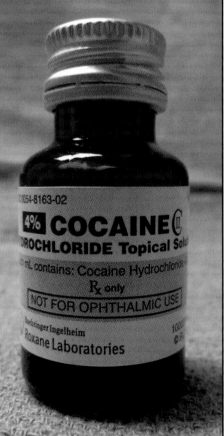

This cocaine is in liquid form.

blew $100,000 on coke in only six weeks. Fed up and scared, Katie left him.

The road to recovery began when Josh showed up at his grandmother's house strung out on crack. He was homeless, dirty, and had lost fifty pounds. A few days before, he had tried to kill himself by swallowing pills. His grandmother took him in and fed him, but when Josh continued to smoke crack, she told him to clean up his act or get out.

"Using drugs behind my grandma's back and being confronted by her, that was my lowest point," Josh said. "But when you feel the most hopeless, you're the most willing to do whatever it takes. That was my moment of surrender."[1]

Like many people, Josh turned to his faith for support in overcoming his addiction. He also went back to rehab and finally got clean. When he got out, he signed on at a faith-based baseball academy called The Winning Inning, in Florida. He cleaned bathrooms, cooked meals, cut grass, and worked with kids to earn time in the batting cage and on the field. Josh stayed there for five months, putting his life back together. He and Katie got back together, too.

When the Tampa Bay team saw the progress Josh had made, they took him back. Josh was eventually traded to the Texas Rangers, where he played for five years, helping them get to the World Series in 2010 and 2011. He is known as a power hitter who is fast in the outfield and has one of the strongest arms in the American League.

Although Josh never failed another drug test, he did relapse twice by drinking alcohol. He now has an "account-ability partner." This is a chaperone hired by his baseball team who lives with him on the road and makes sure he stays strong and sober. Josh is also tested for drugs three times a week to keep him accountable in his fight against relapsing on this powerful drug.

In 2008, Josh published a book about his addiction and recovery, called *Beyond Belief.* These days, he gives inspirational talks to groups on how he overcame his addictions. A movie is also being planned about his life.

What Are Cocaine and Crack?

Cocaine (coke) is a fine, white powder. When cocaine is mixed with hardening substances, it becomes a solid rock, called crack. Crack varies in color from white, to yellow, to pale rose.

Cocaine is usually inhaled (snorted) through a nostril or mixed with water and injected into a vein through a needle. It can also be swallowed or rubbed on the gums. Crack is heated in a pipe and the vapors are inhaled. Both drugs produce a feeling of euphoria—a blissful, excited, self-confident state.

Cocaine occurs in nature. It's extracted from the leaves of the coca plant, which is grown mostly in the Andes Mountains of South America. For thousands of years, native tribes there have chewed coca leaves or made coca tea as a medicine or as part of religious rituals. Using the plant this way is not known to cause addiction, and the euphoria is mild.

Most cocaine is manufactured near the fields where the coca plant is grown. Turning coca leaves into cocaine involves a complicated process of heating and cooling,

Cocaine is extracted from coca leaves.

using several chemicals. Most of the cocaine in the world is controlled by drug cartels from Colombia, South America. However, the drug is usually smuggled into the United States by Mexican gangs.

After drug dealers in the United States buy the powdered form of cocaine, they often deceive addicts by adding cheaper substances, such as cornstarch, talcum powder, or sugar. This makes the cocaine go farther so the dealers make more money. Desperate addicts may sell everything they own to buy what they believe to be pure cocaine. Sometimes, other illegal drugs are added to cocaine, for example, amphetamines or heroin. Some dealers also operate "cook houses" where they turn powdered cocaine into crack.

Cocaine has been classified as a Schedule II drug by the U.S. Food and Drug Administration. This means it has a high potential for abuse but also has legal uses and can be prescribed by a doctor. Cocaine is occasionally used as a local anesthetic during eye, ear, and throat surgeries. Crack has no legal uses.

Impact on the Brain

Cocaine and crack belong to a class of drugs called stimulants. Stimulants speed up the activity in the central nervous system, causing people to feel wide awake, energetic, upbeat, and mentally alert. Cocaine is the most powerful central nervous system stimulant found in nature.

Not all stimulants are illegal or bad for you. Caffeine is one example of a legal stimulant that is generally safe in moderation. It's found in coffee, tea, energy drinks, soft

The Name Game

Some nicknames or "street" names for cocaine are C, snow, flake, blow, sneeze, and nose candy.

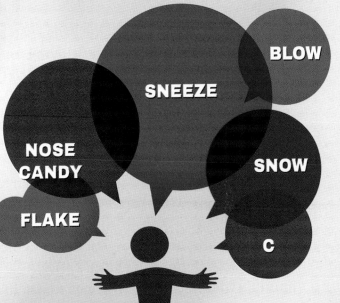

Street names for crack include base, badrock, crunch and munch, electric kool-aid, and devil drug.

drinks, and chocolate. Caffeine keeps you awake, so people drink it in the morning, when studying for exams, when driving, or at other times when they need to stay alert.

Most people know how caffeine affects them. For example, one or two cups of coffee or one energy drink might make them feel perky. But more than that might make them feel jittery, cause their heart to pound, or keep them from sleeping. In rare cases, people have even died from ingesting excessive amounts of caffeine or mixing caffeine products with alcohol. Still, compared to cocaine and crack, caffeine is a very mild stimulant with few risks. Take these caffeine-related side effects and risks and multiply them many, many times to get an idea of what you're up against if you take cocaine or crack.

Cocaine and crack are powerfully addictive. They give a feeling of euphoria—also called a "high" or a "rush"—by changing the way the brain works. The drugs enter the blood and head straight to the nerve cells in the brain. There, they totally confuse an important brain chemical called dopamine, which controls feelings of pleasure. Both drugs cause dopamine to build up in spaces between the nerve cells, so people experience an extra strong sense of pleasure for a short time until the drug wears off.

People who take cocaine or crack regularly need more and more of the drug to experience the same desirable effects. This is called building up a tolerance. After the high wears off, users often feel depressed and edgy. This makes them crave even more of the drug. Using is no longer about feeling good. Now, it's about avoiding the suffering that comes from withdrawal.

Caffeine in soda, chocolate, and coffee helps some people stay awake and alert. Too much caffeine, though, can make a person jittery.

Impact on the Body

Cocaine and crack can destroy a person's health. The drugs narrow blood vessels and increase blood pressure and heart rate, which can damage the heart muscles, coronary arteries, and blood vessels. They can also cause heart attacks and strokes. A 2012 report from the American Heart Association (AHA) showed that regular cocaine use permanently makes arteries stiffer, raises blood pressure, and makes heart muscles thicker. Older people who already have diseased coronary arteries and diseased blood vessels in the brain are at even higher risk.

Even scarier, young people with no history of heart problems can die of heart attacks after using cocaine. Even one use can be fatal.

"It's so sad, we are repeatedly seeing young, otherwise fit individuals suffering massive heart attacks related to cocaine use," said Gemma Figtree, the researcher who led the AHA study. "It's the perfect heart attack drug."[2]

Cocaine and crack can cause many other physical problems, including sleeplessness, loss of appetite, anxiety, fatigue, and irritability. High doses or long-term use can cause twitching, itching, dental problems, stomach and intestinal problems, aggressive behavior, and paranoia–the feeling that people are out to get you. Mixing cocaine with alcohol or other drugs increases the risk of serious side effects or death.

Cocaine and crack users are also at increased risk for catching infectious diseases, such as HIV/AIDS and hepatitis C. They endanger themselves by sharing contaminated needles and by having unprotected sex when they're high. When they're on coke or crack, all their senses are on overdrive. Everything seems to look, taste, sound, and feel better. Users are full of energy and their minds feel razor sharp. Unfortunately, this is just an illusion. While high, people often make very foolish decisions and don't think about the consequences.

Startling Statistics

According to the AHA, cocaine kills more than 15,000 Americans every year. Some of them die from physical problems caused by the drug, and others die from car accidents and other drug-related accidents.[3]

The National Survey on Drug Use and Health found that in 2008, about 1.9 million Americans had used cocaine in the past month and about 359,000 of them were crack users. People aged eighteen to twenty-five used cocaine more often than other age groups.[4]

A 2012 survey of teen attitudes and drug use indicated that 2.7 percent of twelfth graders had used powdered cocaine in the past year and 1.2 percent had used crack. The good news is that, as of the publishing date of this book, the use of both forms of the drug has declined over the last decade.[5]

The Ripple Effect

Cocaine and crack affect more than the people who use them. Families where a parent or older child is a coke or crack addict are in constant upheaval. The other children in the family are scared and confused. When they are old enough to understand about addiction, they have the worry that their parent or sibling will end up in jail or die. Marriages often end in divorce when the sober parent leaves to protect themselves and the children.

Communities are affected by cocaine and crack. When drugs are sold on the street, violence and crime erupt. Homelessness increases, with people losing their jobs and homes due to drug abuse.

Cocaine use also affects hospitals and doctors. According to the National Institute on Drug Abuse, 422,896 Americans who had taken cocaine went to hospital emergency rooms in 2009 with bad side effects.[6] Many cocaine users also need treatment for deadly diseases, such as HIV/AIDS and hepatitis C.

The Road to Recovery

If only there was a "good" drug that addicts could take to wipe out their craving for coke and crack. Unfortunately, no such drug exists, but several drugs show promise. Right now, inpatient and outpatient rehabilitation programs are the most successful modes of treatment. Twelve-step programs, such as Cocaine Anonymous and Narcotics Anonymous, also help people stay clean and sober after they leave treatment by giving them the support of others who are recovering addicts.

Some people, like Josh Hamilton, need many trips to rehab before they stop using cocaine or crack. Even then, staying clean is a daily struggle. Not everyone is lucky enough to have an accountability partner like Josh has. But with hard work and the help of support groups, family, and friends, people can overcome their addictions.

Chapter 2

CENTURIES
of Cocaine

Did you know that cocaine is one of the oldest natural drugs in history? It was first found in the leaves of coca plants that grew in the Andes Mountains of South America, especially in Colombia, Peru, and Bolivia. The Native Americans of that region have been chewing coca leaves for at least five thousand years. Many of them still do. They also brewed the coca leaves in an herbal tea called "mate de coca," which is still popular today.

Cocaine is an alkaloid stimulant, like caffeine and tobacco. An alkaloid is an organic substance found in plants. People in the Andes don't actually chew the coca leaf. They wad it into a ball and add a lime paste made from rock or shells. The lime paste is an alkali that helps release the cocaine from the leaf. They place the wad

Native Americans make a tea from coca leaves. The tea is called *mate de coca*.

(called a quid) into their mouth between their teeth and their cheek. Their saliva then dribbles over the coca leaf, releasing the cocaine down their throat.

To the Incas of Peru, the coca plant was a gift from the gods. They burned or smoked parts of the plant during religious rituals. They also used it as a medicine to treat everything from toothaches to stomachaches. Coca was an important part of daily life. It gave people energy when they were tired and kept them from feeling hungry. Living in the higher altitudes of the Andes was difficult, and coca made it easier to breathe the thin mountain air.

The people of the Andes used coca in moderation— that is, until the Spanish invaded during the 1500s. The Spanish forced the natives to work as slave labor in silver mines up in the mountains. Conditions in the mines were unbearable. The hours were long, food was scarce, and many of the natives died. To increase production and keep fatigued workers motivated, the Spanish gave them a steady supply of coca. You might say the Spanish were the first drug dealers.[1]

Cocaine Is Isolated

For the next three centuries, the people of Europe heard about the amazing qualities of the coca plant, but most never got to try it. The plant and its leaves didn't travel well back then. In 1860, the German chemist Albert Niemann got hold of enough coca leaves to isolate the active ingredient for the first time. He called it cocaine. In its powder form, cocaine was purer and much more powerful than chewing on coca leaves. It was usually

A native Peruvian woman prepares coca leaves for chewing.

· ·

mixed with water or some other liquid and taken orally. At first, the drug companies didn't jump to produce cocaine powder. It was another twenty-five years before it became popular.

Meanwhile, the Italian chemist Angelo Mariani had an idea. Why not combine coca leaves with wine? Vin Mariani appeared around 1870. It didn't contain much cocaine, but it was a big hit with artists, musicians, politicians, and scientists. Even Thomas Edison, Queen Victoria, and Pope Leo XIII endorsed it! A century later, researchers discovered that mixing cocaine with alcohol produced cocaethelyne, a compound almost as stimulating as cocaine by itself. Maybe that's why Vin Mariani was so popular. It was like getting a double dose! [2]

A Magical Drug

One of the early fans of powdered cocaine was a young Austrian doctor named Sigmund Freud. (You may have heard of him. He's known as the founding father of psychoanalysis.) In 1884, Freud wrote a paper about cocaine. He described it as a magical drug that could be used for depression, indigestion, and asthma. He also claimed it could treat morphine and alcohol addiction. Sadly, the people who used it ended up trading one addiction for another.

Freud (and other scientists) also noticed that cocaine had a numbing quality that might make it a good anesthetic. Karl Koller, a doctor who was a friend of Freud, proved that cocaine's ability to deaden feeling made it

Coca helped people breathe the thinner air in the high mountains of Peru. Shown here is Machu Picchu, a fifteenth-century Inca site located on a ridge in Peru.

Angelo Mariani

This poster showing Pope Leo XIII advertised how Mariani wine quickly restored health, strength, energy, and vitality.

an excellent candidate for eye surgery. It was also found helpful for nose and throat surgeries.

During that time, surgeries were brutal. Only ether and chloroform were used and they weren't very effective. People believed that pain was something you had to endure. With the invention of hypodermic syringes, though, doctors found that injecting cocaine could relieve pain during surgery. The demand for the drug soared and so did its production and sales.

William Halsted, an American doctor, began his own research on cocaine injections. He pioneered the use of cocaine as a local anesthetic. Halsted discovered that injecting cocaine directly into nerves would block a nerve and prevent pain in that area. Halsted transformed the world of anesthesia—at the cost of his own health.

It was not uncommon for doctors during the 1800s to experiment on themselves and their coworkers with new drugs. Freud took cocaine to relieve his depression and abused it for many years before he gave it up. Koller put cocaine drops in his own eyes to see how it worked. Halsted injected himself and his coworkers with the drug. As a result, he and many of his coworkers became cocaine addicts. Halsted sometimes couldn't perform surgeries because of it.

The First Epidemic

Doctors weren't the only ones who abused cocaine. By the late 1800s, it was advertised in Europe and the United States as a cure-all for just about anything. Fatigue, headaches, toothaches...you name it. It was included in many patent

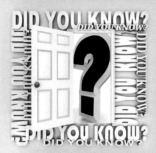
COCAINE
in Coca-Cola?

It's true. After Mariani created his wine, he had many imitators. One of them was John Pemberton, an American pharmacist. In 1886, he invented Coca-Cola® by combining (among other things) extract of kola nut for caffeine, extract of coca leaves, and sugar. Without the sugar, the cocaine would have made the drink very bitter. Coca-Cola was mixed with carbonated water and sold at drugstore soda fountains everywhere. In the early 1900s, cocaine was removed from the formula, but the Coca-Cola company continued to create that special "coke" flavor by adding an extract of coca leaves from which the cocaine was removed.

medicines and tonics. Cocaine toothache drops promised children "instantaneous cure." Throat lozenges with cocaine were labeled "indispensible for singers, teachers, and orators." [3] These "quack" medicines weren't regulated and often included large amounts of alcohol. Meanwhile, doctors recommended cocaine for anxiety and depression, while some people used it as a recreational drug.

Few people wanted to see the dark side of cocaine. In fact, little was known about how cocaine actually affected the body. By the early 1900s, news about the side effects of its use could no longer be avoided. Not just doctors, but respected members of society had become cocaine addicts. Some patients died from unsafe cocaine use during surgeries. Others died from heart attacks or strokes brought on by cocaine. Then the situation got worse. People started snorting cocaine—absorbing powdered cocaine through their nasal passages. By 1910, people were showing up in hospitals with nasal damage. According to some estimates, Americans consumed as much cocaine in 1906 as they would during the next epidemic fifty years later—with half the population! [4]

The United States Congress decided that cocaine needed to be regulated. The Harrison Narcotic Act of 1914 banned the non-medical use of cocaine, prohibited it from being imported, and imposed criminal penalties for users. The popularity of cocaine declined dramatically. New and better drugs were found to replace it as an anesthetic. With reduced supplies of cocaine, only a few people continued to snort or swallow or shoot it for the next few decades. Cocaine was considered a problem of the past . . . for a time.

Cocaine Rises from the Ashes

By the late 1960s, recreational drug use had become more acceptable. People were experimenting with drugs. They were ready for a new fling with cocaine. In 1970, though, the Controlled Substances Act classified cocaine as a Schedule II substance. That meant it had a legitimate medical use but a strong potential for abuse or addiction. The public (and many doctors) disagreed. Other drugs had serious side effects, but cocaine seemed to be relatively harmless. People had forgotten its past history.

Cocaine was all the rage in the 1970s. The "baby boomers" born in the 1940s and 50s were now young adults. They had tried marijuana. Cocaine was the next logical step. Most saw it as a recreational drug they could snort on occasion. Cocaine was easy to use and seemed to be safe. Supplies were limited and the drug was pricey. But if you had a good job, you could afford it. Soon celebrities, like Mick Jagger and Steven Tyler, were using cocaine. It became a "party" drug. Stores sold handbooks on cocaine use. Gold coke spoons hung from chains around people's necks.

The Second Epidemic

In the early 1980s, everything changed. Large cartels took over the production of cocaine. Its manufacture and trafficking became a multibillion dollar business. According to the Drug Enforcement Administration (DEA), the amount of cocaine entering the United States doubled and tripled during the early to mid-1980s.[5] The drug was

A 1900 illustration shows the inside of a drugstore, with many drugs available for purchase.

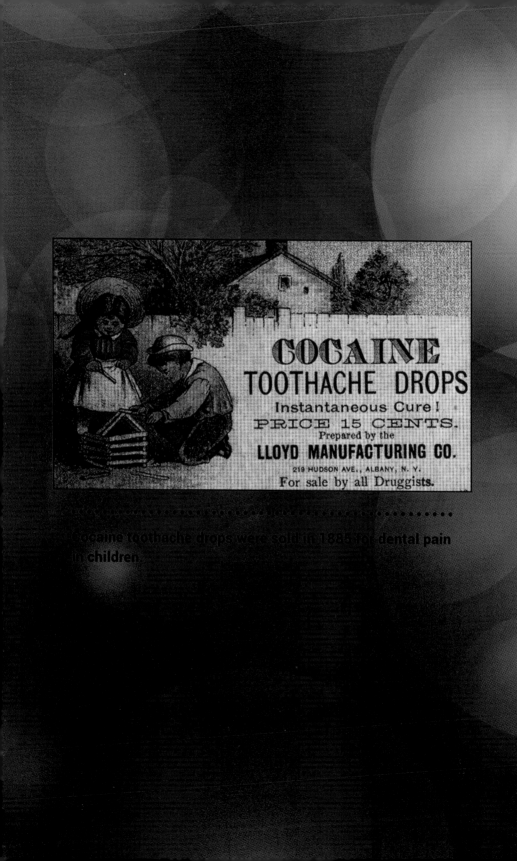

Cocaine toothache drops were sold in 1885 for dental pain in children

not just more affordable. It was also purer, which made it more dangerous.

With cocaine more available, people began to experiment with different ways to use it. One method was called "freebasing." It involved cooking cocaine in water with ammonia and ether. The result was flakes of cocaine you could inhale from a pipe. Smoking cocaine freebase gave an intense rush—more intense than snorting. By the late 1970s, it was the trendy thing to do in Hollywood. But the process was dangerous. In 1980, a famous comedian named Richard Pryor caught fire while cooking freebase and almost died.

A safer technique was found. It involved cooking the cocaine in a simple solution of baking soda and water. The result was not as pure as freebase but you could smoke it in a pipe. It could also be sold in small chunks that made a crackling noise when smoked. It came to be known as "crack."

Dealers could sell chunks of crack cheaply in glass vials or plastic containers. Cocaine was now available to people who didn't have much money. Larger and purer batches of drugs were smuggled in from the cartels in South America. By the mid-1980s, crack was being sold in poor and working class neighborhoods all over the country.

Cocaine soon showed its dark side once again. Gangs moved in on the crack trade. A wave of street and property crime followed. Turf wars between gang members ended in many deaths. Some were innocent bystanders. As addiction rates increased, so did health

THE Turning Point

In 1986, Len Bias was a star basketball player at the University of Maryland. Some people thought he was as good as Michael Jordan. On June 17 of that year, he was the number two overall pick in the NBA draft by the Boston Celtics. Len never got to play for them.

On the morning of June 19, Len was talking to a friend. He suddenly collapsed and had several seizures. Len was taken to the hospital but never regained consciousness. A few hours later, he was pronounced dead from cardiac arrhythmia. Traces of cocaine were found in his urine.

People's attitudes about cocaine and crack changed. If someone as young and healthy as Len Bias could die from cocaine use, it was obviously not a safe drug. Len's death triggered a war on drugs that became controversial.

Former University of Maryland basketball star Len Bias poses in his college uniform.

· ·

problems. Trading sex for drugs contributed to the spread of HIV/AIDS and hepatitis C.

The cocaine epidemic lasted from the 1970s to the mid-1990s. One study estimated that at the peak, as many as 8 million Americans may have used cocaine or crack regularly. Of that number, 5 to 8 percent had a serious addiction. By the mid-1980s, crack cocaine had replaced heroin as the main illicit drug problem in the United States.[6]

The War on Drugs

The death of Len Bias in 1986 stunned the nation. Drugs now became a political issue. Congress had passed The Anti-Drug Abuse Act in October of the same year. The bill set aside $1.7 billion to fight a war on drugs. It also mandated minimum penalties for drug offenses. Prisons were soon filled with people arrested for minor drug offenses.

Crack was seen as a more serious problem than powder cocaine so the penalties for crack were harsher. These penalties have been criticized over the years for promoting racial inequality in the prison population. In 1994, the United States Sentencing Commission found that sentences for crack were mostly imposed on African Americans. Convictions for cocaine offenses were more racially mixed.[7] In 2010, The U.S. Congress finally passed the Fair Sentencing Act, which reduced the inequality between sentences for crack and cocaine violations.

Has the war on drugs succeeded? Since 1988, cocaine use has declined among casual users. Crack also has become less popular. That's good news. But eliminating the cocaine market is an uphill battle. Many professionals believe that cocaine abuse should be treated as a health issue, not a crime. They want to emphasize prevention and treatment rather than enforcement. As more studies are done, more effective strategies emerge to help people win their own war against cocaine. Meanwhile, the history of cocaine will continue to warn us about the danger of being too optimistic.

Chapter 3

COCAINE
on the Brain

Seventeen-year-old Tom Bertram snorted up to sixty lines of cocaine a day for three months. It cost him about $330 per week. Then it almost cost him his life.

The British teenager tried coke for the first time on his seventeenth birthday, after three years of smoking pot. "Coke gave me such a buzz, and I liked the confidence it gave me. I never considered the risks," he said."[1]

That confident feeling ended on a terrifying note. After three months on coke, Tom suddenly collapsed in agony while riding in the car with his mother. She rushed him to the hospital, where the doctors fought to save his life. Tom's heart was beating at only one-third of its normal rate. He was having a massive heart attack, and the doctors suspected it was from abusing drugs.[2]

Tom survived the heart attack, but his heart and coronary arteries were permanently damaged. The doctors had to insert a battery-operated pacemaker in Tom's chest to keep his heart beating normally. He'll have to wear the pacemaker under his skin near his heart for the rest of his life. The scar and lump on his chest are constant reminders of how close he came to dying.[3]

Now in his early twenties, Tom is a successful musician and songwriter who has cut an album and toured in Europe. But he'll never forget how cocaine almost killed him.[4]

"I know I'm lucky to be alive," he said. "I regret putting my family through so much heartache. I feel like I've been given a second chance and I'm determined to use it.[5]

It's not cool to have a pacemaker at seventeen," Tom admitted.[6]

What Is Drug Abuse? Dependence? Addiction?

Drug abuse is an intense desire to use more and more of a drug until it takes over your life and replaces normal activities.

Drug dependence means a person has a physical need to take a drug in order to function normally. It occurs because your body gets used to the drug. Abruptly stopping the drug leads to withdrawal symptoms. These range from depression and other mental problems to physical problems like vomiting. It all depends on the drug.

Drug addiction is a brain disease that drives a person to use a drug, even though he knows it has harmful effects. People use more than intended, pay a price they didn't mean to pay, and yet continue to use the drug despite devastating consequences. Addiction is a chronic condition, like diabetes. That is, addicts are never "cured" but must manage their condition over their lifetime. Cocaine is so powerful, people who stop taking the drug may still crave it years later. That's why so many people relapse or return to using.

It's possible to have a physical dependence on a drug without being addicted to it. For example, people take medicine to lower blood pressure, and their bodies get used to it. If they stop taking the medicine, their blood pressure goes up. But these drugs don't change the brain and the people aren't addicted.

Some sources say cocaine and crack cause addiction but not physical dependence. Not everyone agrees. This theory probably arose because withdrawal symptoms from cocaine and crack are mainly emotional, not physical. People who suddenly stop using the drugs feel depressed and anxious, but they don't necessarily vomit or shake like those withdrawing from alcohol or some other drugs. That's why it's easy to fool yourself into thinking you aren't addicted to cocaine.

Some researchers believe that all addiction starts in the brain. In other words, there's no such thing as physical addiction or mental (psychological) addiction. There's just addiction. Since the end result is the same, this theory is probably closer to the truth.

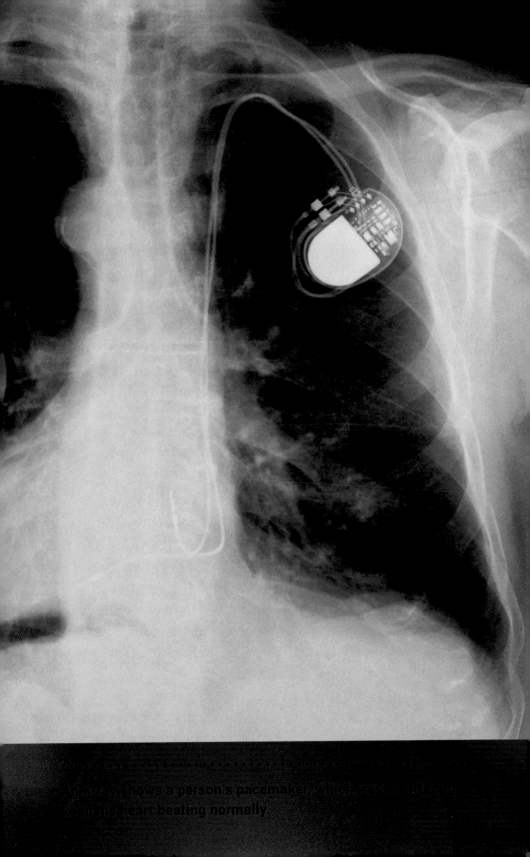

An X-ray shows a person's pacemaker, which was inserted to keep his heart beating normally.

A person with an addiction is called an addict. Besides drugs, people can also become addicted to substances, such as tobacco or food. Or they can become addicted to behaviors, such as shopping or gambling. Many people have more than one addiction. For instance, they may be addicted to both alcohol and cocaine or to gambling and shopping at the same time.

The Brain's Reward Pathways

Why are cocaine and crack so addictive? Researchers have studied the brain, looking for answers. They discovered a "reward pathway" in the center of the brain that contains millions of nerve cells. This pathway controls behavior, motivation, and pleasure. It tells us to eat, drink, have sex, and engage in other behaviors that ensure our survival and the survival of the human race.

Think about it: If food had no taste or tasted nasty, would we bother to eat? Probably not! But if we stopped eating, we'd die. With the help of the five senses, the brain protects us by saying "Yes!" as soon as we bite into that slice of pepperoni pizza. This message travels to the nerves in the reward pathway. There, it triggers the release of the chemical dopamine, which is stored in the brain's nerve cells. Dopamine floods out of the cells and floats around in the synapses, the open spaces between nerve endings.

Across the synapses, in the receiving nerve cells, dopamine receptors are waiting. These receptors are like locks and dopamine is the key. When dopamine fits into these locks, we feel pleasure. That's why dopamine is

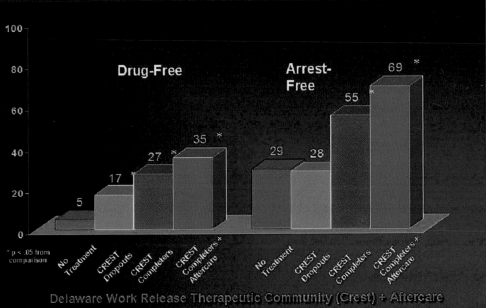

Treatment Reduces Drug Use and Recidivism

Drug-Free

Arrest-Free

* p < .05 from comparison

No Treatment — 5
CREST Dropouts — 17
CREST Completers — 27 *
CREST Completers + Aftercare — 35 *

No Treatment — 29
CREST Dropouts — 28
CREST Completers — 55 *
CREST Completers + Aftercare — 69 *

Delaware Work Release Therapeutic Community (Crest) + Aftercare
Drug-Free and Arrest-Free 3 Years After Release (N=448)

Source: Monitoring the Future.org, 2013

called the "feel-good chemical." But pleasure isn't meant to last forever, so the dopamine is eventually shuttled back to the sending nerve cells to be stored and used later. Extra dopamine is destroyed.

The reward pathway makes us repeat feel-good behaviors by connecting to other parts of the brain that control memory and behavior. It tells the brain, "Atten-SHUN! This is important. Remember it."

Your Brain on Cocaine

All drugs, even legal ones, affect the brain. But drugs of abuse, like cocaine and crack, actually change the way the brain works. How? They short-circuit the nerve cells so they don't communicate properly. Nerve cells "talk" to each other by releasing chemicals called neurotransmitters. These chemicals latch onto the nerve cells at receptor sites.

Dopamine is a very important neurotransmitter. It controls feelings of pleasure and pain in the brain and body. It also affects movement. But cocaine seriously messes up dopamine. Normally, dopamine is ejected from a nerve cell in response to something pleasurable—like the smell of cookies baking. Then it hitches a ride on protein transporters and is recycled back to the cell that released it. The dopamine rests there until the next time it needs to be used.

Cocaine blocks dopamine re-uptake. That's the technical term. Here's how it works: Cocaine shoves dopamine out of the way so it can't attach to the transporters. Then it hijacks the transporters back to the releasing nerve cells

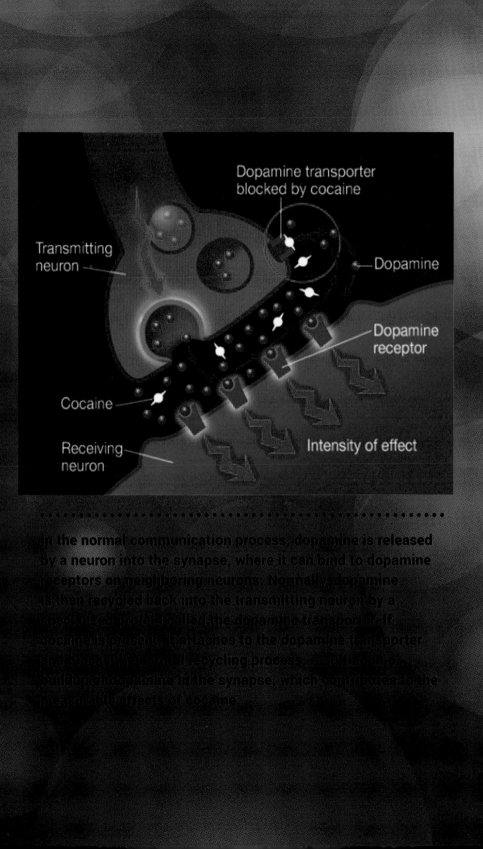

In the normal communication process, dopamine is released by a neuron into the synapse, where it can bind to dopamine receptors on neighboring neurons. Normally, dopamine is then recycled back into the transmitting neuron by a specialized protein called the dopamine transporter. If cocaine is present, it attaches to the dopamine transporter and blocks the normal recycling process, resulting in a buildup of dopamine in the synapse, which contributes to the pleasurable effects of cocaine.

WAYS TO TAKE
Coke and Crack

The route of administration always predicts how quickly the user experiences the effects of the drug. Freebasing (smoking) cocaine is the fastest route to the brain. However, the most common way to take powdered cocaine is by snorting it. People pour the powder onto a mirror or other flat surface and then use a razor blade to crush the powder and separate it into "lines." They inhale the drug by inserting a straw or rolled-up paper money into a nostril. The drug is absorbed into the bloodstream through the tissues in the nose. People feel high in ten to fifteen minutes, and the high lasts up to thirty minutes. Rubbing cocaine onto the gums has a similar effect.

Powdered cocaine can also be mixed with water and injected into a vein using a needle and syringe. The drug goes directly into the bloodstream, so the high occurs faster and is more intense. But it only lasts five to ten minutes.

Crack is smoked in a small glass pipe called a "straight shooter." A piece of steel wool at one end of the pipe tube acts as a filter. A piece of crack is placed on the other side of the filter. When the crack is heated, it produces a vapor, or smoke, which is inhaled into the lungs.

The drug enters the bloodstream and reaches the brain in only ten to fifteen seconds, much faster than inhaled powder cocaine. The high is very intense, but it only lasts five to fifteen minutes. This makes crack very addicting, because people are always chasing the next high.

and stays there a long time. This leaves dopamine hanging out in the synapse, where it keeps bouncing back to the nerve cell receptors like a ball in a pinball machine. Every time the dopamine hits the receptor, it gives the body another jolt of pleasure. That's why someone on cocaine or crack feels so fantastic and full of energy.

Your Brain *Off* Cocaine

Unfortunately, those awesome feelings don't last. Our bodies aren't meant to feel such intense pleasure. The brain can't handle it, so it protects itself by reducing the number of dopamine receptors. This decrease shows up clearly on the brain scans of coke and crack addicts. Are these brain changes permanent? Are brain cells dormant (inactive) or actually damaged? Researchers are still sorting out these questions.

With fewer receptors, the brain becomes less responsive to cocaine. Instead of feeling pretty normal after the drug wears off, users feel depressed and restless. This makes them take more cocaine or crack, trying to recapture those first feelings of pleasure. This is also called "chasing a high." With continued use, the highs get lower and the lows get deeper. People develop a tolerance to the drug. This is what happened to Tom Bertram.

If someone who has been using a lot of cocaine stops taking it abruptly, he goes into withdrawal. He may be agitated, restless, irritable, and tired. He may feel severely depressed, even suicidal. Other withdrawal symptoms include increased appetite, unpleasant dreams, and slowing of activity. In other words, the opposite of a high.

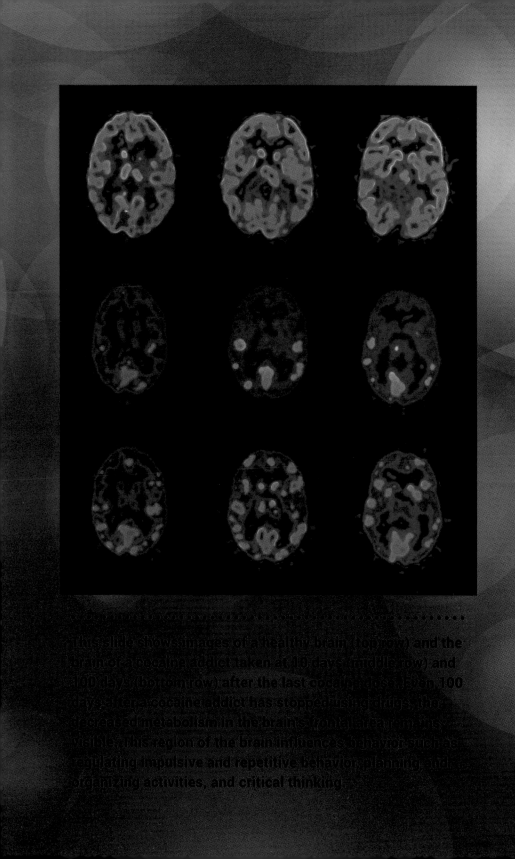

This slide shows images of a healthy brain (top row) and the brain of a cocaine addict taken at 10 days (middle row) and 100 days (bottom row) after the last cocaine dose. Even 100 days after a cocaine addict has stopped using drugs, the decreased metabolism in the brain's frontal area remains visible. This region of the brain influences behavior such as regulating impulsive and repetitive behavior, planning and organizing activities, and critical thinking.

Signs of Cocaine and Crack Abuse

Tom Bertram's mom didn't realize he was abusing cocaine. But if she had known what to look for, she may have recognized the telltale signs. Here are the clues that someone is abusing cocaine or crack:

Behavior Changes: Abusers often lose interest in school or in their jobs, giving up sports, social activities, and hobbies. Their personalities change and they become irritable, moody, secretive. and get angry for no reason. Abusers may miss meetings, family gatherings , not show up for work or school on a regular basis. They abandon friends and hang out with other drug users.

While high, people become excited, talkative, energetic, and unable to sit still. If they stay high, they lose their appetite and hardly sleep. Bingeing can lead to a mental state much like schizophrenia, called cocaine psychosis. People become paranoid and hallucinate (see and hear things that aren't there).

Physical Signs: Abusers may lose weight and stop caring about their appearance. If they snort coke, they may have a constantly runny nose, stuffiness, or crusting around the nose. People who smoke crack may have burns on their fingertips and singed eyebrows and eyelashes. They may be short of breath and cough up black mucus. People who inject cocaine usually have needle marks on their arms or other parts of their bodies

Metal spoons, lighters, and needles are used to take cocaine.

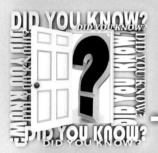

DRUG
Money

Your mother may have warned you that money's dirty, so wash your hands after handling it. But she probably never dreamed that it might be contaminated with cocaine.

About 90 percent of paper money circulating in the U.S. and Canada contains traces of cocaine, according to a study done at the University of Massachusetts in Dartmouth. The powder form of coke gets on the bills when money is exchanged during drug sales. It also gets on bills that are rolled up and used to snort coke.

The drug was detected on the bills by examining them with a device called a gas chromatograph-mass spectrometer. The study concluded that the amount of coke on money isn't enough to make someone high.[7]

Environmental Clues: Cocaine and crack users, especially teens, usually try to hide their drug use from family members. Telltale signs include rolled-up dollar bills or bits of white powder on flat surfaces, such as books or mirrors. Other drug paraphernalia include razor blades, crack pipes, metal spoons, wet cotton, and needles and syringes. Money or valuables may be missing from the house because the user has taken them to pay for drugs.

Drugs of Deception

Cocaine and crack are devious drugs. A single dose, or even two or three doses, won't make someone an addict. But addiction sneaks up gradually, especially if the drugs are readily available and affordable.

Cocaine and crack are unpredictable drugs. Even low doses can kill. One reason is because the body becomes ultrasensitive to the drugs' toxic effects. People have died of heart attacks immediately after one hit of cocaine. Other people take the drug one hundred times and then drop dead the next time. There is no relationship between the number of uses and the chance of your heart stopping.

Cocaine and crack are not drugs to take lightly.

Chapter 4

COCAINE, CRACK, and Their Consequences

Christina Huffington was pretty, smart, and grew up in a wealthy family that loved her. But the Yale University student was living a secret life. Alone in her dorm room, she was snorting cocaine six or seven times a day.[1]

She first tried cocaine when she was only sixteen.[2] She said it made her feel euphoric, confident, and beautiful.[3] After that, she was hooked. She got high with her friends, at home doing her homework, and at school in the bathroom. One day, the housekeeper found Christina's stash of coke. Devastated, Christina's mother began taking her to the doctor for random drug tests.[4]

After that, Christina managed to go "cold turkey." That is, she stopped using cocaine abruptly. She concentrated on school and got into Yale. Then, her second year of college, she saw another student doing coke and figured she could handle it just one time. She ended up hooked again. A serious nosebleed scared her into quitting again, and she stayed clean through her third year of college. She even held down a summer job at a fashion magazine. Then she found out her former boyfriend was dating her friend, and she did coke the first night of her senior year. After that, she used the drug almost every day for three months straight.[5]

Christina lost weight, started skipping classes, and ditched her closest friends. She stopped answering her mother's phone calls. She lied to her friends and family.[6] Then one night in March 2012, Christina stayed up all night snorting coke and then smoked pot. Suddenly, she couldn't breathe, and she ended up in the emergency room. That was the turning point for her.[7]

With her family's support and professional help, Christina is now drug free.[8] She returned to Yale to finish her degree.[9] She hopes her story will help other young people struggling with addiction.

"I know there are thousands of those girls out there, feeling like I did: alone, isolated, and guilty. I want to tell them that getting through it is possible. And once you do get through it, you have a life," she said.[10]

Your Body on Cocaine

As coke and crack travel through the blood, they impact the body as well as the brain. Organs can be damaged permanently. The extent of damage depends on the person's general health, how much of the drug is taken,

Christina Huffington and her mother, Arianna Huffington, attended *Glamour* magazine's 2013 Women of the Year in New York City.

how long the person has been using, and other factors. The route of administration, or how the drug is taken, is also important. Here's how coke and crack affect the body:

Nose: People who snort coke heavily lose their sense of smell and have nosebleeds and a constantly runny or stuffy nose. They may have sinus problems and facial pain. Cocaine can actually perforate (eat holes through) the nasal septum—the dividing wall between the nostrils. This is known as "coke nose" and causes a whistling sound when the person breathes. Worse yet, the nose may become permanently deformed and collapse.

Lungs: Smoking crack irritates the lungs and can lead to chronic bronchitis; coughing up black, nonbloody phlegm; shortness of breath; chest pain; and collapsed lungs.

Heart: Both drugs make the heart beat abnormally. It may go too fast, too slow, or beat irregularly. The drugs also make blood pressure spike up and arteries narrow down, so blood has trouble reaching the heart. This can cause a heart attack, even in young, healthy people.

Kidneys: Cocaine and crack can overload the kidneys with toxins (poisons) and cause them to shut down suddenly.

Digestive system: Both drugs narrow the blood vessels feeding the stomach and intestines, giving them less oxygen. Oxygen starvation can cause severe irritation and perforations in the stomach or intestines. Swallowing cocaine cuts off the blood flow so drastically, intestinal gangrene can occur, causing the intestines to die. Heavy

A LETHAL Combination

People who abuse cocaine or crack often take them along with other drugs. Taking two or more psycho-active (mood-altering) drugs at the same time or within a short timeframe is called polydrug use, and it's highly dangerous. Why? Because drugs that might not kill you if taken alone can form deadly combinations in the body.

Alcohol and cocaine or crack are especially lethal. Taken together, they combine in the liver to form coca-ethylene, a third, deadly substance. This substance inten-sifies cocaine and crack's euphoric effects. The National Institute on Drug Abuse calls alcohol and cocaine/crack the most common two-drug combination that results in drug-related deaths.[11]

The combination of alcohol and cocaine can be deadly.

users may also stop eating regularly, causing severe weight loss and malnutrition.

Skin: Injecting cocaine causes needle puncture marks or "tracks," usually in the forearms. The injection sites can become infected. People can also get hepatitis C or HIV/AIDS from sharing needles. Heavy users may imagine that bugs are crawling on or under their skin ("coke bugs") and scratch themselves raw.

Sex life: Coke and crack, like other drugs, make people lose their inhibitions so they're more likely to have unprotected sex or sex with multiple partners. This increases their risk for sexually transmitted diseases. Heavy use can cause men to have trouble getting erections or ejaculating.

Teeth: Cocaine and crack use can lead to tooth grinding, which causes tooth enamel to wear away. Rubbing cocaine on the gums can make them dry, which leads to cavities.

Body temperature: Both drugs can cause hyperthermia, a dangerous increase in body temperature. At the same time, people lose the ability to cool down or even realize they're too hot. Hyperthermia can cause brain damage, failure of the heart and other organs, coma, and even death.

Cocaine Overdose

How much cocaine or crack is lethal? That's hard to say. Some people have died after snorting just one line of coke.

Overdose symptoms are terrifying. People may have stabbing headaches, pounding heartbeats or barely any heartbeats at all, severe muscle cramps, loss of muscle

Cocaine use causes many side effects in the body.

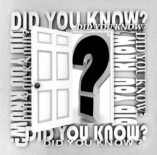

A DEADLY *Harvest*

Cocaine starts out innocently enough. It comes from coca plants, which grow naturally in Peru, Colombia, and Bolivia, South America. Peasant farmers produce up to six crops a year and pick the leaves by hand. Then they begin the illegal process of turning the leaves into paste.

Cocaine is made by a complicated process of heating, cooling, and adding chemicals. Making the paste is the first of three steps. Farmers use water, sodium carbonate, and kerosene to produce the putty-like, white or light-tan paste. The process includes stomping on the leaves. They then sell the paste to drug cartels who continue the manufacturing process.

The second step is converting the coca paste into cocaine base. This is done in "base labs" located deep in the jungle and requires more complicated equipment. Some chemicals involved include sulfuric acid, hydro-chloric acid, and ammonia. The resulting mixture is dried with heat lamps and becomes cocaine base.

The third and final step is converting the base to cocaine hydrochloride. This process requires a bigger facility; more equipment; and more dangerous, flammable chemicals, including acetone. The result is the cocaine powder that is sold on the street.

Crack is easy to make. It involves dissolving cocaine powder in water and baking soda. Then the mixture is boiled to separate the solid from the liquid. It's cooled, dried, and cut up into small nuggets or rocks. Drug dealers convert powder cocaine to crack after the powder is smuggled into the country, usually across the Mexican border.

control, and confusion. They may have several seizures in a row and lose consciousness or go into a coma. Some suffer strokes, heart attacks, and die.

A condition known as excited delirium can also occur, causing sudden death. People shout but don't make sense, become violent and combative, and are extremely paranoid, hyperactive, and unusually strong.

If a coke or crack user shows any of these signs, call 911 so the person can be taken to the emergency room immediately!

"Crack Babies"—Reality or Myth?

As crack use increased in the 1980s and 1990s, the news media began printing horrifying stories about "crack babies." These were babies whose mothers took crack while pregnant. Babies were reported to be permanently brain damaged and have severe physical defects.

More recent studies have shown that this was an exaggeration. Researchers have studied children whose mothers took cocaine or crack during pregnancy, and years later, most of these children are no worse off than children whose mothers didn't. Most babies exposed to these drugs don't have birth defects

Does this mean it's safe to use cocaine or crack while pregnant? No! The drugs can cause miscarriage—having the baby too early for it to survive. They can cause the placenta to separate from the uterus, causing severe bleeding and killing both mother and baby. They can also cause premature babies who are born too early and underweight. Underweight babies are more likely to die in their first month of life.

Cocaine decreases the amount of oxygen the unborn baby gets. So even full-term babies are often small and have abnormally small heads. Newborns may have sleeping problems due to cocaine withdrawal. Older children may have learning and language problems and sight and hearing defects. They may also be aggressive and have trouble paying attention.

Coke and crack can cause all these problems. But the fact is, many other issues must be taken into account. For example, was the pregnant woman smoking, drinking alcohol, or taking other drugs, too? Did she get good medical care while pregnant? Did she eat properly? Did she have a sexually transmitted disease?

Women on coke or crack often take several other drugs, which is known as polysubstance abuse or dependence. They don't generally go to doctors, eat right, sleep enough, or take care of their health. They also neglect their children and expose them to dangerous living conditions. Chances are, if an infant or child has problems, exposure to cocaine or crack before birth is only one of many causes.

Legal Penalties for Cocaine and Crack

Possessing or selling crack and cocaine is illegal in all fifty states. But until a few years ago, the penalties for crack were one hundred times more severe than for the same amount of cocaine!

How did this happen? When crack appeared on the scene in the mid-1980s, politicians and the news media called it the most addictive drug known to man. They blamed it for violent crimes and deformed babies. They warned that crack use would spread from the cities to the suburbs. These notions were all exaggerations.

Back then, people thought crack was a totally different drug than powder cocaine, and way more addictive. They didn't understand crack was simply the base form of the powder. Today, we know that both drugs are strongly addictive, and the differences aren't all that noteworthy.

So the American Civil Liberties Union and other civil rights organizations were furious when the U.S. Congress passed strict sentencing laws in the 1980s. These laws made the sale or possession of five grams of crack punishable with five years in prison. Dealers who sold five hundred grams of powder coke got the same penalty! People holding large amounts of crack ended up with life in prison without parole. Most of them were poor African-American men from the inner city. This is not surprising, because the poor are often more at risk than others for drug abuse. Many of these people were first-time offenders with no history of violent crimes.

These laws changed in 2010, with the passage of the Fair Sentencing Act. Now, the penalty for crack has been lowered to eighteen times what it is for powder cocaine. However, many people, including judges, think the penalties should be the same for both drugs.

Other Legal Consequences

Crack is the only illegal drug carrying a mandatory (fixed) sentence of at least five years in prison. People caught with powder cocaine usually get off easier. First-time offenders may get probation and no jail time, but their lives may still be changed forever.

A drug conviction may stay on a person's record for the rest of his or her life. Legal consequences can be severe and may include paying steep fines and losing your driver's license. A drug conviction can disqualify you for scholarships or student loans for college. It can also affect your ability to get a good job. Most employers run criminal background checks to be sure people don't have problems that might affect their work or put other workers at risk. Certain jobs will also be out of bounds, such as working for the police department, owning a liquor store, or driving a truck or taxi. A felony drug charge will also mean you can't own a gun, and you may be denied a visa to travel to foreign countries. Cocaine and crack can change people's lives. And none of the changes are good ones.

Chapter 5

FACING THE TRUTH
About Coke and Crack

In 1981, *Time* magazine wrote an article about cocaine, referring to it as "the all-American drug."[1] It was also an expensive drug. That's partly what attracted many respectable people in the middle class to use it. Cocaine was a symbol of upward mobility. They also believed it was safe to use. But cocaine had a dark side, as people soon discovered.

Diana grew up in an upper-middle-class home and started to use cocaine in high school. Where did she get the drug? Not on the streets, but in the homes of her friends' parents, where it was readily available.

The more Diana used cocaine, the more she craved it. It wasn't long before she needed it to survive. Her mom knew her daughter abused alcohol, but she never guessed she would use cocaine. Still, Diana's drug use was affecting their family. And Diana's dad, who was divorced from her mom, also used cocaine. He saw no problem with his daughter using it, too.

Diana finished school and got a great job, but cocaine affected her work. She was using the drug morning, noon, and night. Some days she didn't even make it to work. After a time, she began to have serious health issues and was always broke.

Finally, a friend convinced her to get help and took her to a twelve-step meeting. That twelve-step program helped turn her around. So did her mom's support. Diana got another job, moved, and found new friends. She even avoided her father until he finally stopped doing coke and got sober, too.[2]

The Lure of Cocaine

No one starts using a drug intending to become a drug addict. People often intend to try it once, maybe twice because they're curious, or because they want to seem cool and go along with the crowd. But as time passes, the drug begins to take control of the user. It's no longer a matter of free choice. People who are addicted will do anything to get the drug. That's what happened to Diana. It didn't help that society at the time didn't believe that cocaine was really dangerous or addictive. After all, if rich, so-called "respectable" people used it, it must be harmless, right?

There are many influences on people, especially teens, to try cocaine and other drugs:

Teens often use drugs for the first time when they feel peer pressure.

Celebrities and sports figures are often role models that young people respect. When these idols use drugs, they give the message that it's not just acceptable. It's "cool."

Parents or caregivers who use drugs are sending a message that it's okay. It's no surprise that kids whose parents use drugs are more likely to use them, too. Studies show children of users also use drugs at an early age and are more likely to become dependent.[3]

Peer pressure is a major influence. Teens often get drugs for the first time from a sibling or friend. It may be someone they admire or want to hang out with. Or maybe they feel bullied into trying drugs.

The Internet is a great source of information about drugs, especially government Web sites like *NIDA for Teens* and *Just Think Twice*. But the Internet is also a source of misinformation. Messages on social networking sites, like Facebook, and tweets about illicit drug use can tempt kids to try drugs.

Today's movies, music, and advertising often send out a positive message to kids about drug use. The more they hear about it, the more they're curious about trying. The bad effects of drug use is often not displayed or is downplayed.

Why Teens Choose Cocaine

Young people are especially at risk for doing cocaine. Why do some teens decide to try it? There's no single reason. Everyone's different. But there are a few common factors that experts have noticed.

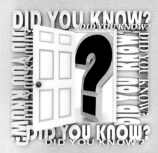

THE "CELEBRITY" *Drug*

Sports icons, supermodels, musicians, and actors have tried cocaine. Some have stopped, others have damaged their lives and careers, and a few have died as a result.

Super Bowl winner Lawrence Taylor has been arrested more than once for trying to buy cocaine. Baseball superstar Dwight Gooden abused cocaine throughout his career. He was given a prison sentence for using it in 2006.

Supermodels Kate Moss and Naomi Campbell both admitted to using cocaine at one time. They each claim to be sober now.

Musicians have used cocaine, too. Steven Tyler said that his need for cocaine took his marriage and his children away. Elton John admitted to wasting a good part of his life on cocaine and considers himself lucky that he got clean. Whitney Houston wasn't so lucky. Cocaine contributed to her death.

The list of movie stars who admit to cocaine use is nearly endless: Angelina Jolie, Charlie Sheen, Drew Barrymore, Dennis Quaid, Robert Downey, Jr., Lindsay Lohan, and Colin Farrell to name a few. Even Oprah Winfrey confessed to using cocaine for a while when she was young.

Amy Winehouse attends court to face assault charges at Westminster Magistrates Court on July 23, 2009, in London, England. It was claimed that the singer hit a fan during an event in London the previous year.

Peer pressure is a factor. So is being exposed to people in your life, like friends or family members, who use drugs. And so is buying into the idea that using cocaine isn't really risky. In Diana's case, cocaine was easily available, which is one more factor.

Did you also know that kids who have a lot of stress are twice as likely to use illegal drugs? Or that teens who are bored are fifty percent more likely to try drugs than kids who aren't?[4] Here are a few more reasons why some teens may be at risk for using cocaine and other drugs:

- **Low self-esteem:** It's not unusual for young people who are still growing socially to lack confidence. Some believe that taking cocaine will make them feel more confident and secure.

- **Curiosity:** Some teens want to know what it feels like to be "high" from cocaine.

- **Rebellion:** It's normal for teens to feel rebellious at times. Some kids use drugs to rebel because they know society and their parents would disapprove.

- **Creating an image:** Some kids believe that doing a drug like cocaine will make them appear more mature or sophisticated.

Being at risk doesn't mean you'll become a drug user. But you can never be sure. So if you feel pressured or tempted to try drugs, stop and think for a minute. Maybe you should share your concerns with an adult you trust—a friend, teacher, parent, or relative. You may even want to seek counseling. Drugs don't make problems go away.

THE COCAINE *Myth*

One of the myths about cocaine is that it's safe. How many adults today even know about the dangers of cocaine use? And how many parents, who experimented with it when they were young, have too casual an attitude about it? Cocaine, like so many other drugs, is about denial.

Diana's dad didn't want to admit his daughter was an addict. It would have meant admitting he was an addict, too. Diana's mom couldn't believe her daughter would use a drug like cocaine. If they both hadn't been in denial, perhaps Diana would have gone into recovery sooner.

They just hide them for a while. Sooner or later those problems show up, waiting for you to deal with them.

A Family Disease

Cocaine controls the lives of people who are dependent on it. More than that, like all drugs, it controls the lives of the people around them. Cocaine abuse is especially devastating to families. It becomes the focus of everyone's life. Family members all feel anger, resentment, fear, concern, and guilt. They are forever suspicious that the addict is using. They feel hurt when the addict spends so much time on drug use and withdraws from family activities. Money becomes an issue because drug habits are so expensive.

Without realizing it, family members often enable the addict's drug use. They might deny there's a serious drug problem. They may make excuses for the addict's behavior or lend her money to pay bills. Family and friends often do this out of love, but it keeps the addict from dealing with problems caused by her addiction.

The good news is that families can break free from the grip of cocaine addiction. Getting support from a therapist trained in drug dependency is one way. Another is to go to a twelve-step program, like Co-Anon or Nar-Anon, where families and friends of addicts can share experiences and learn to cope with their difficulties. Most treatment programs consider family members a vital part of the addict's recovery. It's really the "family" working toward recovery.

Above all, families need to know they are not responsible for someone else's addiction. If they stop enabling the addict, educate themselves about cocaine abuse, and do what they can to get help for the addict, they may be able to turn things around.

Kicking the Coke Habit

Drug addiction in teens is different from adult addiction. Teens are still developing mentally, physically, and emotionally. Their brains continue to grow until their early twenties. Using cocaine can interfere with its development. A teen on drugs can't think clearly or make good decisions. She might lose interest in school, lie, steal, or have sex—something she wouldn't do otherwise.

Drug abuse on a developing brain can cause what scientists call "developmental arrest." It means a young person's physical and emotional development stops until he becomes sober. For example, a person who uses drugs at thirteen can stay emotionally stuck at that age. As a young adult, he may still have poor judgment or be unable to judge the consequences of his actions.

Being in the right program will improve a teen's chance of recovery. He needs treatment that responds to his unique needs. Family support is vital. So are academics, feedback from peers, and age-appropriate therapy. It's also critical for parents to be involved in treatment. As a general rule, treatment should begin with the least restrictive option and move up, if needed.

Detox is the first step. Detox involves getting the drug completely out of the body. An addict who stops using

The right rehab program will increase a person's chance at recovery.

cocaine may not have physical symptoms. But he will still have symptoms, like fatigue, depression, and an intense craving for the drug. They can be so overwhelming the addict might give up before he starts. He may also have other drugs in his system. Getting help at a detox center is a good idea so the addict can have round-the-clock observation and support. If that's not possible, it's best to call a healthcare provider for help. Going through detox alone is not easy and those withdrawing from stimulants can be at increased risk for suicide.

Rehab is where the actual treatment takes place. Inpatient and outpatient programs are both available, depending on the specific needs of the addict. Early inter-vention (outpatient) programs work with teens during the first couple years of use. A mix of individual, family, and group therapy may be offered, as well as one to ten hours of therapy a week. Residential (inpatient) programs are for teens with complications from abuse or unstable homes. It's also for those who have relapsed after several attempts at outpatient programs. Both of these programs should be geared to the unique needs of a teen addict. They should also include frequent drug testing both during and after rehab.

Self-help programs have helped people with addiction problems by keeping them from relapsing both during and after rehab. Twelve-step programs, like Cocaine Anonymous (CA) and Narcotics Anonymous (NA), offer guidance and encouragement to people in recovery. SMART Recovery (not a twelve-step program) teaches people to cope with their urges and manage their feelings

LAST TWO DECADES OF ALCOHOL, CIGARETTE, AND ILLICIT DRUG USE*

*Past 30 day use.

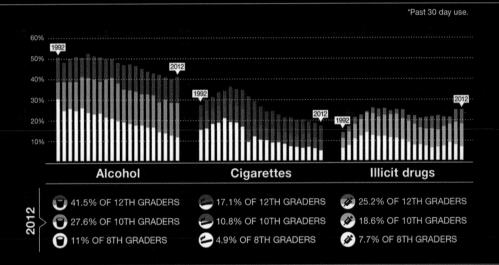

	2012					
Alcohol	41.5% OF 12TH GRADERS	Cigarettes	17.1% OF 12TH GRADERS	Illicit drugs	25.2% OF 12TH GRADERS
	27.6% OF 10TH GRADERS		10.8% OF 10TH GRADERS		18.6% OF 10TH GRADERS
	11% OF 8TH GRADERS		4.9% OF 8TH GRADERS		7.7% OF 8TH GRADERS

NIH National Institute on Drug Abuse

The National Institute on Drug Abuse is a component of the National Institutes of Health, U.S. Department of Health and Human Services. NIDA supports most of the world's research on the health aspects of drug abuse and addiction. Fact sheets on the health effects of drugs of abuse and information on NIDA research and other activities can be found at www.drugabuse.gov.

and behaviors, in a safe environment. All three have programs for teens. The best part? It's the chance to connect with people who understand what you're going through because they've been there, too. No one can do it alone.

It's important to mention that self-help programs are not a substitute for detox and treatment. But they are an important support, both during and after treatment, in reducing the addict's chance of using again. Changing your lifestyle is a key to avoiding drug problems from occurring again. Going through rehab, then hanging out with old drug-using friends almost guarantees a relapse. If someone wants to stop using cocaine, he needs to make some life changes.

- ◆ Stay away from drug-using people and places.

- ◆ Make friends with people who don't use drugs.

- ◆ Don't let yourself get bored. Find new activities to fill the time you spent doing cocaine.

- ◆ Avoid risky situations or feelings that led you to using.

- ◆ Find ways to reduce stress in your life.

- ◆ Surround yourself with a support group of people you can go to when you're feeling weak or tempted.

Recovery from cocaine abuse and addiction isn't easy, but it can be done.

Chapter 6

CRACKING THE
Cocaine Challenge

Mark grew up in a middle-class, New England home. His father took good care of him but was very controlling. He always found fault with everything Mark did. "I felt as if I could never do anything right," Mark said. "No matter what I did, it never was enough to please my dad."

Mark didn't start using drugs until he was around seventeen. Like many other teens, he began with pot and alcohol. By the time he was eighteen, he was getting drunk. But booze alone didn't do it for him. Cocaine did. He started snorting coke in his early twenties and loved it. It gave him the feeling of confidence he lacked because of his father's constant criticism.

"My dad told me I would probably flunk out of college," he said. "When I graduated 43rd out of a class of 950, my dad said that meant 42 kids did better than me. When I started my own business, he said I would probably blow all the money I made." No matter what Mark achieved, he never felt good enough.

Once Mark started to use cocaine, he couldn't stop. It became an obsession. He didn't just snort one line. He would do it over and over again. When his nose started to bleed from snorting, he learned how to do freebase and smoke it. As Mark's addiction got worse, his business went downhill. With less money for cocaine, Mark started using the cheaper crack mixed with other dangerous drugs. In the end, it affected his mind. He became psychotic.

"It's a progressive disease," said Mark. "At first, it starts out a lot of fun. But after a while, it makes you really paranoid."

Mark started hearing voices and seeing demons. He found himself hiding in closets and peeking out of windows. Mark looked horrible. His family and friends worried about him. He tried several times to get clean from cocaine but would relapse after a couple of months. "It always started with a drink," he said.

Then it happened. At first he thought he was having a heart attack. He was wrong. It was a cocaine seizure. He fell violently to the floor and couldn't stop shaking. It was Mark's wakeup call. His business was bankrupt. His customers were leaving and so were his employees. The pain he felt from using was worse than the pain he felt from getting clean.

Mark has been clean from alcohol and cocaine for four years. That's how long he's been going to AA and

NA meetings. It wasn't until he put his recovery before anything else that he succeeded. He also believes that his faith in a higher power has made a difference.

"I'm lucky to be alive," he said. "A lot of my friends weren't as fortunate."[1]

The Cost of Cocaine

Mark's story shows how coke and crack can destroy people. It also ruined his business and impacted the people who worked for him. But the terrible effects of cocaine and crack use are even more far-reaching. Drug abuse costs society billions every year. It affects education, the economy, the health system, the justice system, and the environment. How? The list is nearly endless:

◆ Spousal abuse and divorces

◆ Loss of financial stability

◆ Lost work time and inefficiency in the workplace

◆ Drugged driving and auto accidents

◆ Visits to hospital emergency rooms for misuse of drugs

◆ Addiction treatment for drug abuse

◆ The destruction of South American rain forests for the planting of coca fields

Cocaine use even affects the safety of nations. Some terrorist organizations raise money through drug production and trafficking.

The cost of drug abuse on society is billions of dollars a year, including emergency room visits and auto accidents. This accident resulted from substance abuse. All three teens had been drinking.

Is the War on Drugs a Success?

Yes and no. From 2001 to 2011, there was over a 70 percent drop in pure cocaine production in Colombia, which supplies 95 percent of the cocaine that reaches the United States.[2] From 2002 to 2011, the number of first-time cocaine users fell from one million to 670,000. First-time crack users decreased from 337,000 to 76,000.[3] Prison populations have also begun to drop.

But the problem isn't over yet. A percentage of those first-time users could become addicted. And the cocaine and crack addicts who started using in the 1970s and 80s are still a huge burden on society. Meanwhile, our prisons are filled with small-time crack users given long mandatory sentences because of the Anti-Drug Abuse Act passed in 1986.

The war on drugs gave billions of dollars to police, prisons, and the military in order to suppress all drug use. The emphasis was on putting addicts away, not treating them. That's because during the 1980s, people thought drug abusers simply lacked the willpower to go straight. Thanks to advances in science, attitudes have changed.

A Twenty-first Century Approach

Today's science shows that addiction is a disease of the brain. But there is hope. It's also a preventable disease that can be treated successfully. In 2013, the Office of National Drug Control Policy (ONDCP) announced a new drug strategy based on scientific evidence. Its focus would be more on health care than law enforcement. The plan was to help people who are limited by drug use to overcome their

addiction and take their place in the global community.
The new National Drug Control Strategy includes:

◆ Expanding national and community programs to
educate young people in schools and in the workplace about drugs.

◆ Training healthcare professionals to recognize the
early stages of substance abuse and to intervene
before addiction develops.

◆ Expanding access to treatment. Only one in ten
addicts actually gets the treatment he needs. The
new Affordable Care Act will require insurance
companies to cover treatment for addiction as a
chronic disease.

◆ Identifying non-violent drug offenders and
providing them with treatment instead of prison.

◆ Creating programs to help guide former offenders
back into society and support their recovery from
addiction.

The government will still focus on disrupting drug
production and trafficking in the United States. It will also
continue to work with other nations to do the same.[4]

The Science of Prevention

Prevention is the best way to fight cocaine abuse,
especially when it comes to young people. Research shows
that the longer teens go without using drugs, the less
likely they are to get addicted. It also shows that teens
won't start using a drug if they understand how harmful it

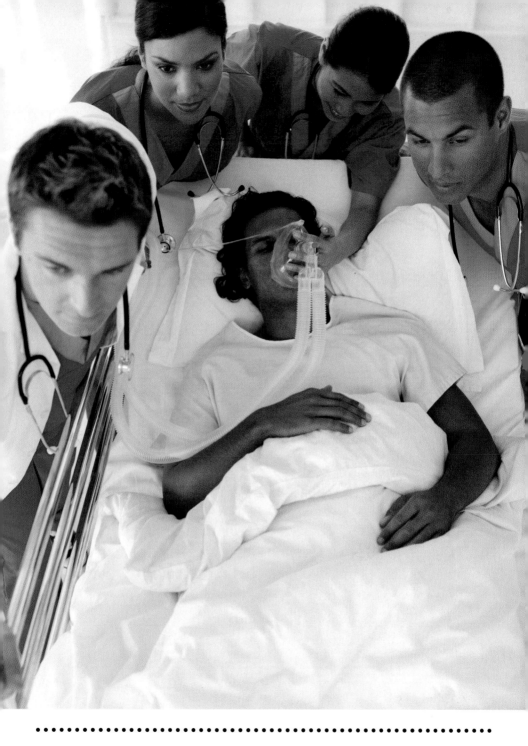

Prevention is the best way to fight drug abuse, to prevent people from hurting themselves and ending up in the emergency room, or worse.

can be. Prevention programs based on scientific research like this actually reduce drug abuse. The National Institute on Drug Abuse (NIDA) supports three types of prevention programs:

1. **School programs** are aimed at specific groups of young people, such as middle school students. They educate kids about the effects of drugs and ways to resist them.

2. **Family programs** target high-risk youth and their families. Programs offer information about drug abuse symptoms, teach parenting skills and provide family therapy.

3. **Community programs** reach out to youth in general. They advertise trends in drug use and explain social skills.

Saying "no" to drugs isn't easy, especially when other kids pressure you. But did you know that most kids don't want to try drugs? That's right. You're in the majority. Maybe it's time to let people know what you think. Hold an after-school discussion about drugs, sponsor a drug-free day at school, or get trained to be a peer counselor and help other kids with problems. Peer pressure can be a positive thing when it encourages kids to be responsible.

The Science of Treatment

Treating drug abuse is a lot harder than preventing it in the first place. There's no one-size-fits-all treatment for cocaine addiction. Many addicts also abuse alcohol or other drugs. They may be suffering from mental health

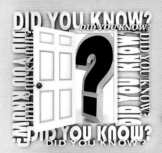

THE TEEN BRAIN
on Cocaine

Statistics show that the risk of drug abuse and addiction is much higher when cocaine use begins during the teenage years. A study done with mice at Yale University in 2012 may explain why.

Research shows that the teen brain is shifting from growing to becoming more settled like an adult's. That's what makes it more susceptible to cocaine addiction. When a teenage brain is exposed to cocaine through a pathway regulated by integrin beta1, it tries to defend itself by changing the shape of the nerve cells and synapses. Integrin beta1 is a gene that is essential in the development of the nervous system.

In the latest study, when researchers blocked the pathway and prevented the cells from changing, the mice were three times more sensitive to the effects of cocaine. Locating this gene may also help explain why some people get addicted to cocaine and others don't.[5]

Therapists work with teens and family members to improve communication during drug counseling.

problems, too. The best treatment meets the individual needs and problems of an addict, especially if he's a teenager.

Finding a qualified professional is essential. It's also important to choose a counselor who specializes in addiction. Not every mental health provider understands addiction, although some addiction counselors may have credentials in mental health, too. Here are some therapies that researchers say work:

Cognitive Behavioral Therapy (CBT): CBT has helped to decrease cocaine use and prevent relapse. The theory is simple. Cocaine abuse and addiction is a learned behavior. Why shouldn't the same learning process help people stop using? Patients learn to recognize the situations when they're likely to use cocaine. Then they're taught ways to avoid those situations and to cope with the behaviors that drug abuse creates.

Multidimensional Family Therapy (MDFT): MDFT works well for young people. This therapy treats teen drug abuse as a complex issue that includes personal problems, relationships, and family. Therapists work with teens and their parents separately and in joint sessions. Patients learn techniques to reduce conflict, improve communication, and strengthen family bonds. The system is flexible and can be used in community clinics, residential treatment centers, correctional facilities, and even clients' homes.

Multisystemic Therapy (MST): MST is an intensive treatment for chronic juvenile offenders who may also be drug addicts. It is an outpatient, home-based therapy.

IS CIGARETTE SMOKING A "GATEWAY" TO Cocaine Abuse?

The results are in. In a study at Columbia University, a group of mice were given water with nicotine while a control group drank plain water. Seven days later, all the mice were injected with cocaine for four days. In the end, the mice receiving nicotine were 78 percent more likely to return to areas associated with cocaine.

Does that apply to people, too? The researchers analyzed data from a national study. They found that people who were smokers when they first used cocaine were more likely to be dependent than people who never smoked or stopped before they first used. That means nicotine probably sensitizes people's brains to the addictive effects of cocaine. Next on the researchers' list to study? Alcohol.[7]

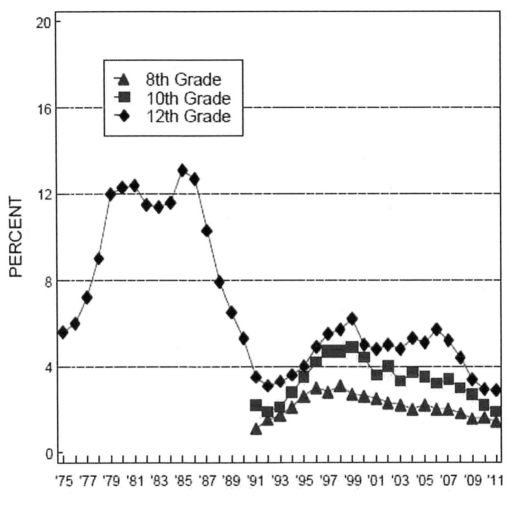

This chart shows the percent of students who have used illegal drugs between 1975 and 2011. The report is from the Substance Abuse and Mental Health Services Administration. Results from the 2012 National Survey on Drug Use and Health: Summary of National Findings.

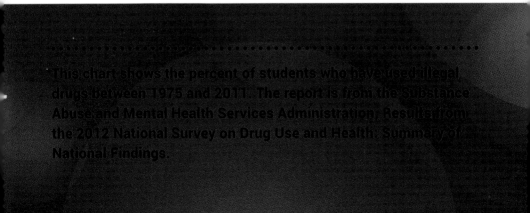

MST targets the issues in a teen's environment that may contribute to his drug abuse—homes and families, schools and teachers, neighborhoods and friends. Therapists work in teams with small caseloads and are available twenty-four hours a day, seven days a week if needed.

Can a Vaccine Stop Coke Addiction?

No medications are available yet to treat cocaine addiction. There is exciting research being done on a cocaine vaccine, though, which shows promise. One method is to attach a chemical similar to cocaine to a virus. It's hoped that the body will develop a natural immunity to the chemical. When cocaine is introduced to the body, antibodies will then prevent the cocaine from reaching the brain. There are some studies in clinical trials, but it will probably be years before a vaccine will become available.[6]

Science has made a big difference in dealing with drug abuse. It's shown us that addiction is not a moral weakness but a disease of the brain that can be treated and possibly even cured. It's also shown us ways to prevent more cocaine abuse in the future. Young people are smart. When they hear the facts, they know how to make the right choices.

Chapter Notes

Chapter 1 — A POWERFUL Stimulant

1. Mike DiGiovanna, "The Fall and Rise of Josh Hamilton," *The Aberdeen News*, February 4, 2013, <www.aberdeennews.com/sports/la-sp-0205-josh-hamilton-addiction-20130205,0,278269.story> (March 12, 2013).

2. "Recreational Cocaine Use Linked to Conditions That Cause Heart Attack," American Heart Association Meeting Report, November 5, 2012, <http://newsroom.heart.org/news/recreational-cocaine-use-linked-239564> (March 25, 2013).

3. "Cocaine, Marijuana and Other Drugs and Heart Disease," American Heart Association, <www.heart.org/HEARTORG/Conditions/Cocaine_UMC_428537_Article.jsp> (March 25, 2013).

4. "Cocaine: Abuse and Addiction. What Is the Scope of Cocaine Use in the United States?" National Institute on Drug Abuse, <www.drugabuse.gov/publications/research-reports/cocaine-abuse-addiction/what-scope-cocaine-use-in-united-states> (February 18, 2013).

5. "Monitoring the Future, 2012 Survey Results," National Institute on Drug Abuse, <www.drugabuse.gov/related-topics/trends-statistics/infographics/monitoring-future-2012> (March 28, 2013).

6. "Drug-Related Hospital Emergency Room Visits," National Institute on Drug Abuse, <www.drugabuse.gov/publications/drugfacts:drug-relatedhospitalemergencyroomvisits> (March 27, 2013).

Chapter 2 — CENTURIES of Cocaine

1. Steven B. Karch, *A Brief History of Cocaine*, (Boca Raton, Fla.: CRC Press, 1998).
2. Ibid.
3. "Before Prohibition: Images from the preprohibition era," Addiction Research Unit, Department of Psychology, University at Buffalo, State University of New York, <http://wings.buffalo.edu/aru/preprohibition.htm> (April 15, 2013).
4. "Appendix C: History of Cocaine," *The CIA-Contra-Crack Cocaine Controversy*, United States Department of Justice, December 1997, <http://www.justice.gov/oig/special/9712/appc.htm> (February 11, 2013).
5. "Chapter 1—Introduction," *Treatment for Stimulant Use Disorders*, Substance Abuse and Mental Health Services Administration, 1999, <http://www.ncbi.nlm.nih.gov/books/NBK64337/?report=printable> (February 11, 2013).
6. Ibid.
7. "A Social History of America's Most Popular Drugs," *Frontline: Drug Wars*, PBS, <http://www.pbs.org/wgbh/pages/frontline/shows/drugs/buyers/social history.html> (April 15, 2013).

Chapter 3 — COCAINE on the Brain

1. "Teen Needs Pacemaker After 60 Line-a-Day Cocaine Habit," FoxNews.com, August 12, 2009, <www.foxnews.com/story/2009/08/12/teen-needs-pacer> (November 23, 2013).

2. Julie Moult, "Boy, 17, Fitted with Pacemaker after Massive Heart Attack Caused by £200-a-Week Coke Binge," *Mail Online*, August 21, 2009, <www.dailymail.co.uk/femail/article-1205751/17-year-old-boy-suffers-heart-attack-caused-by-£200-a-week-coke-binge> (April 15, 2013).

3. David Bowden, "Hard-Hitting Ads Target Young Cocaine Users," *Sky News*, October 9, 2009, <www.news.sky.com/story/731093/hard-hitting-ads-target-young-cocaine-users> (April 16, 2013).

4. "Tom Bertram," <www.tombertram.co.uk/about> (November 23, 2013).

5. Moult, "Boy, 17, Fitted with Pacemaker after Massive Heart Attack Caused by £200-a-Week Coke Binge."

6. Bowden, "Hard-Hitting Ads Target Young Cocaine Users."

7. Christine Dell'Amore, "Cocaine on Money: Drug Found on 90% of U.S. Bills," *National Geographic News*, August 16, 2009, <http://news.nationalgeographic.com/news/pf/42217793.html> (April 20, 2013).

Chapter 4 — COCAINE, CRACK, and Their Consequences

1. Eun Kyung Kim, "'Pit of Loneliness': How Arianna Huffington's Daughter Hid Cocaine Addiction," Today.com/news, August 7, 2013, <www.today.com/news/pit-loneliness-how-arianna-huffingtons-daughter-hid-cocaine-addiction> (November 23, 2013).

2. "Arianna Huffington's Daughter: Cocaine Almost Killed Me," Today.com/video, August 7, 2013, <www.today.com/video/today/52693308> (November 23, 2013).

3. Christina Huffington, "Addiction Recovery: Getting Clean at 22," Huffington Post.com, April 13, 2013, <www.huffingtonpost.com/christina-huffington/addiction-recovery-getting-clean> (November 23, 2013).

4. Sophia Banay Moura, "Christina Huffington: Cocaine Almost Killed Me," Glamour.com, September 2013, <www.glamour.com/inspired/2013/08/arianna-huffington-s-daughter-christina-huffington> (November 23, 2013).

5. Ibid.

6. Huffington.

7. Kim.

8. Huffington.

9. Cindi Leive, "Christina Huffington, and her Mom, Arianna, Break Their Silence on Christina's Addiction," August 7, 2013, <www.glamour.com/inspired/blogs/the-conversation/2013/08/christina-huffington> (November 23, 2013).

10. Kim.

11. "Cocaine: Abuse and Addiction. What Are the Short-Term Effects of Cocaine Use?" National Institute on Drug Abuse, <www.drugabuse.gov/publications/research-reports/cocaine-abuse-addiction/what-are-short-term-effects-cocaine-use> (February 18, 2013).

Chapter 5 **FACING THE TRUTH** *About Coke and Crack*

1. Michael Demarest, "Cocaine: Middle Class High," *Time* Magazine, July 6, 1981, <http://content.time.com/time/magazine/article/0,9171,922619,00.html> (November 25, 2013)

2. Vicki D. Greenleaf, *Women and Cocaine: Personal Stories of Addiction and Recovery*, (Los Angeles: Lowell House, 1989).

3. *Get it Straight!: The Facts about Drugs, Student Guide,* Drug Enforcement Administration, 2011, <www.justice.gov/dea/pr/multimedia-library/publications/get-it-straight-student.pdf> (April 15, 2013).

4. Ibid.

Chapter 6

CRACKING THE
Cocaine Challenge

1. Authors' phone interview with Mark S., November 21, 2013.

2. "Survey Shows Significant Drop in Cocaine Production in Colombia," Office of National Drug Control Policy, July 30, 2012, <http://www.whitehouse.gov/ondcp/news-releases-remarks/survey-shows-significant-drop-in-cocaine-production-in-Colombia> (April 24, 2013).

3. *Results from the 2011 National Survey on Drug Use and Health: Summary of National Findings*, Substance Abuse and Mental Health Services Administration, 2012, <http://www.samhsa.gov/data/nsduh/2k11results/nsduhresults2011.htm#5.4> (April 21, 2013).

4. "A Drug Policy for the 21st Century," Office of National Drug Control Policy, April 24, 2013, <http://www.whitehouse.gov/ondcp/drugpolicyreform> (April 24, 2013).

5. "Cocaine and the teen brain: Yale research offers insights into addiction," *Yale News*, Yale University, February 21, 2012, <http://news.yale.edu/2012/02/21/cocaine-and-teen-brain-yale-research-offers-insights-addiction> (February 11, 2013).

6. Jennifer Welsh, "How Cocaine Vaccines Could Cure Drug Addiction," *LiveScience*, June 22, 2012, <http://www.livescience.com/21132-cocaine-vaccine-cure-addiction.html> (April 28, 2013).

7. Lori Whitten, "Nicotine Makes Mouse Brain More Responsive to Cocaine," National Institute on Drug Abuse, February 20, 2013, <http://www.drugabuse.gov/news-events/nida-notes/2013/02/nicotine-makes-mouse-brain-more-responsive-to-cocaine> (April 20, 2013).

Glossary

addiction—A brain disease that causes an uncontrollable dependence on a substance or behavior.

antibodies—Proteins that neutralize a substance introduced into the body.

Anti-Drug Abuse Act—A 1986 bill that set aside $1.7 billion to fight a war on drugs. It also set minimum penalties for drug offenses.

base lab—Also called a "cook house." Facilities deep in the jungles of South America where cocaine paste is converted to cocaine base or the base is converted to cocaine powder.

binge—A long run of uninterrupted drug use. People on coke binges are hyperactive and rarely sleep, but they keep taking the drug to avoid crashing.

coca plant—A plant that grows naturally in the Andes Mountains of South America. Its leaves are used to make cocaine.

cocaethelyne—A third chemical made in the body when alcohol and cocaine or crack are taken together. This intensifies the effects of the drugs and can be deadly.

cocaine—A stimulant drug extracted from the leaves of the coca plant, using a process of heating, cooling, and adding chemicals.

cocaine base—The second substance created in the cocaine manufacturing process.

cocaine paste—The first substance created in the cocaine producing process.

cocaine hydrochloride—The fine, white powder created during the final step in the cocaine manufacturing process. This is what is sold on the street.

cognitive behavioral therapy—An addiction treatment that focuses on changing people's thoughts in order to change their behavior.

coke bugs—The sensation coke addicts have that bugs are crawling on or under the skin.

coke nose—Irreversible damage to the inside of the nose caused by snorting coke. The nose may actually collapse.

crack—Rock-like substance created when powder cocaine is mixed with water and chemicals, then cooled and dried. Crack is smoked in a pipe.

crash—The comedown when someone suddenly stops using a drug like cocaine or crack. Addicts often sleep for days and feel depressed and suicidal.

detox—The abbreviation for *detoxification*, or withdrawing from a drug under medical supervision.

dopamine—The "feel-good" chemical in the brain that makes people feel pleasure.

dopamine receptors—Special sites on the brain's nerve cells that receive dopamine.

drug abuse—An intense desire to use more and more of a drug until it takes over a person's life and replaces normal activities.

drug dependence—When a person has a physical need to take a drug in order to function normally.

euphoria—Extreme happiness, excitement, or feeling of well-being.

excited delirium—A condition caused by cocaine overdose where people shout, become violent, and are extremely paranoid, hyperactive, and unusually strong. Sudden death may occur.

freebasing—A way to smoke cocaine in a pipe that was popular thirty years ago. The cooking process was very dangerous because it used highly flammable chemicals.

hallucination—The experience of having visions; seeing, hearing, or sensing what isn't there.

high—A state of euphoria caused by drugs.

hyperthermia—A very high body temperature. Cocaine overdose can cause this possibly fatal condition.

integrin beta1—A gene that is essential in the development of the nervous system. It may help protect the brain from cocaine when a teen first uses it.

multidimensional family therapy—An addiction treatment for young people that sees teen drug abuse as a complex issue that includes personal problems, relationships, and family.

multisystemic therapy—An addiction treatment for chronic juvenile offenders who abuse drugs. The intensive home-based therapy targets all the issues in a young person's environment that contribute to drug abuse.

neurotransmitter—A chemical released from a nerve cell that transmits a message to another nerve cell. Dopamine is a neurotransmitter in the brain.

overdose—An excessive amount of a drug, more than the body can handle. Cocaine overdose can cause hyperthermia, heart attack, coma, and death.

polydrug use—Using more than one mood-altering drug at the same time.

rehab—Short for *rehabilitation*. An inpatient or outpatient program for drug addicts after detox. It helps them learn to live without the drug and involves both counseling and support groups.

reward pathway—The nerve pathway in the brain that controls motivation, behavior, and pleasure. Addictive drugs can short-circuit this pathway.

Schedule II drug—A drug that has a legitimate medical use but a strong potential for abuse or addiction.

snort—To inhale an illegal drug through the nose.

stimulant—A drug that speeds up the central nervous system and makes people alert and energetic.

support group—A group of people with similar addictions who meet regularly to support each other through recovery.

synapse—The space between nerves.

tolerance—The point where the body has adapted to the drug and now needs a certain amount to feel normal. The drug stops making a person feel high or even very good, if taken in the usual amount. Tolerance occurs with repeated use.

toxic—Poisonous, harmful, or deadly.

transporters—Proteins that shuttle dopamine back to the nerve cells that released it in the brain. Cocaine blocks this action.

withdrawal—The body's reaction to abruptly stopping a drug a person has become dependent on. Some symptoms of cocaine withdrawal include depression and anxiety.

Further Reading

Books

Apel, Melanie Ann. *Cocaine and Your Nose: The Incredibly Disgusting Story*. New York: Rosen Publishing, Inc., 2005.

Bickerstaff, Linda. *Cocaine: Coke and the War on Drugs*. New York: Rosen Publishing, Inc., 2009.

Chastain, Zachary. *Cocaine: The Rush to Destruction*. Broomall, Pa.: Mason Crest Publishers, 2012.

Kuhn, Cynthia, Scott Swartzwelder, and Wilkie Wilson. *Buzzed: The Straight Facts About the Most Used and Abused Drugs from Alcohol to Ecstasy*. New York: W.W. Norton & Company, 2008.

West, Krista and Ronald J. Brogan. *Cocaine and Crack*. New York: Chelsea House Publishers, 2008.

Internet Addresses

National Institute on Drug Abuse (NIDA). NIDA for Teens. © 2013
   <teens.drugabuse.gov>

Office of National Drug Control Policy. National Youth Anti-drug
   Media Campaign. Above the Influence.com © 2013
   <www.abovetheinfluence.com>

U.S. Drug Enforcement Administration (DEA). Get It Straight!: The
   Facts about Drugs, Student Guide. © 2013
   **<www.justice.gov/dea/pr/multimedia-library/publications/get-it-
   straight-student.pdf>**

U.S. Drug Enforcement Administration (DEA). Just Think Twice.
   © 2013
   <www.justthinktwice.com>

Organizations

Co-Anon Family Groups World Services
PO Box 12722
Tucson, AZ 85732-2722
(800) 898-9985
<www.co-anon.org>

Cocaine Anonymous World Services
21720 South Wilmington Avenue, Suite 304
Long Beach, CA 90810-1641
(310) 559-5833
<www.ca.org>

Nar-Anon/Nar-Ateen
22527 Crenshaw Boulevard
Suite 200B
Torrance, CA 90505
(800) 477-6291
<www.nar-anon.org>

Narcotics Anonymous
78 Gough Street
San Francisco, CA 94102
(415) 621-8600
<www.na.org/>

National Institute on Drug Abuse (NIDA)
Office of Science Policy and Communication, Public Information and Liaison Branch
6001 Executive Boulevard
Room 5213, MSC 9561
Bethesda, MD 20892-9561
(301) 443-1124
<www.drugabuse.gov/>

Office of National Drug Control Policy
The White House
1600 Pennsylvania Avenue NW
Washington, DC 20500
(202) 456-1414
<www.whitehouse.gov/ondcp/>

Substance Abuse and Mental Health Services Administration (SAMHSA)
1 Choke Cherry Road
Rockville, MD 20857
(877) 726-4727
<www.samhsa.gov/>

Index

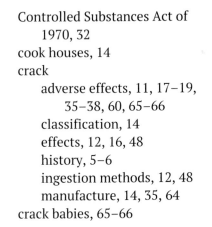